AF251332

RAIN SHADOW

RAIN SHADOW

by James R. Newton · Illustrated by Susan Bonners

Thomas Y. Crowell   New York

Also by James R. Newton

A FOREST IS REBORN

FOREST LOG

THE MARCH OF THE LEMMINGS

Rain Shadow
Text copyright © 1983 by James R. Newton
Illustrations copyright © 1983 by Susan Bonners
Printed in the United States of America.

Library of Congress Cataloging in Publication Data
Newton, James R.
  Rain shadow.

  Summary: Explains how the "rain shadow," or dry,
environment develops on the leeward side of many high
mountain ranges, and contrasts it with the rain forest,
or wetter environment, on the windward side.
  1. Rain shadows—Juvenile literature.   [1. Rain
shadows.   2. Rain and rainfall.   3. Weather, Influence
of mountains on]   I. Bonners, Susan, ill.   II. Title.
QC929.R17N38 1983   574.5'264   82-45927
ISBN 0-690-04344-9
ISBN 0-690-04345-7 (lib. bdg.)

The sun-warmed air is heavy with the moisture it has swept from the surface of the Pacific Ocean.

As it rises higher and higher above the rolling waves, the air cools. Invisible water vapor changes back to tiny water droplets, which form into puffy white clouds.

Least
sandpiper
Glaucous-winged gull

The clouds grow and darken as westerly winds push them steadily toward the shore.

They float over the beaches strewn with driftwood, and the sand dunes dotted with scrubby trees molded in odd shapes by the strong sea breezes.

They sail inland over the top of a great forest of towering evergreen trees. There the clouds climb still higher into the sky as the wind tries to squash them against the steep slopes of the rugged Cascade Mountain Range.

In this higher, colder air they cannot hold all their moisture. The tiny droplets bump into each other and form larger drops.

Then, as it does most days of the year, the rain begins. Down into the lush green forest the raindrops fall, splashing and dripping from branch to branch.

The amount of rainfall the forest receives is so great that green plants grow everywhere. The forest floor is covered with ferns and mosses. Bushes grow from decaying stumps and logs. Tree branches are draped with curtains of greenery. Even the air seems to be green.

Alpine fir
75'
Lupine

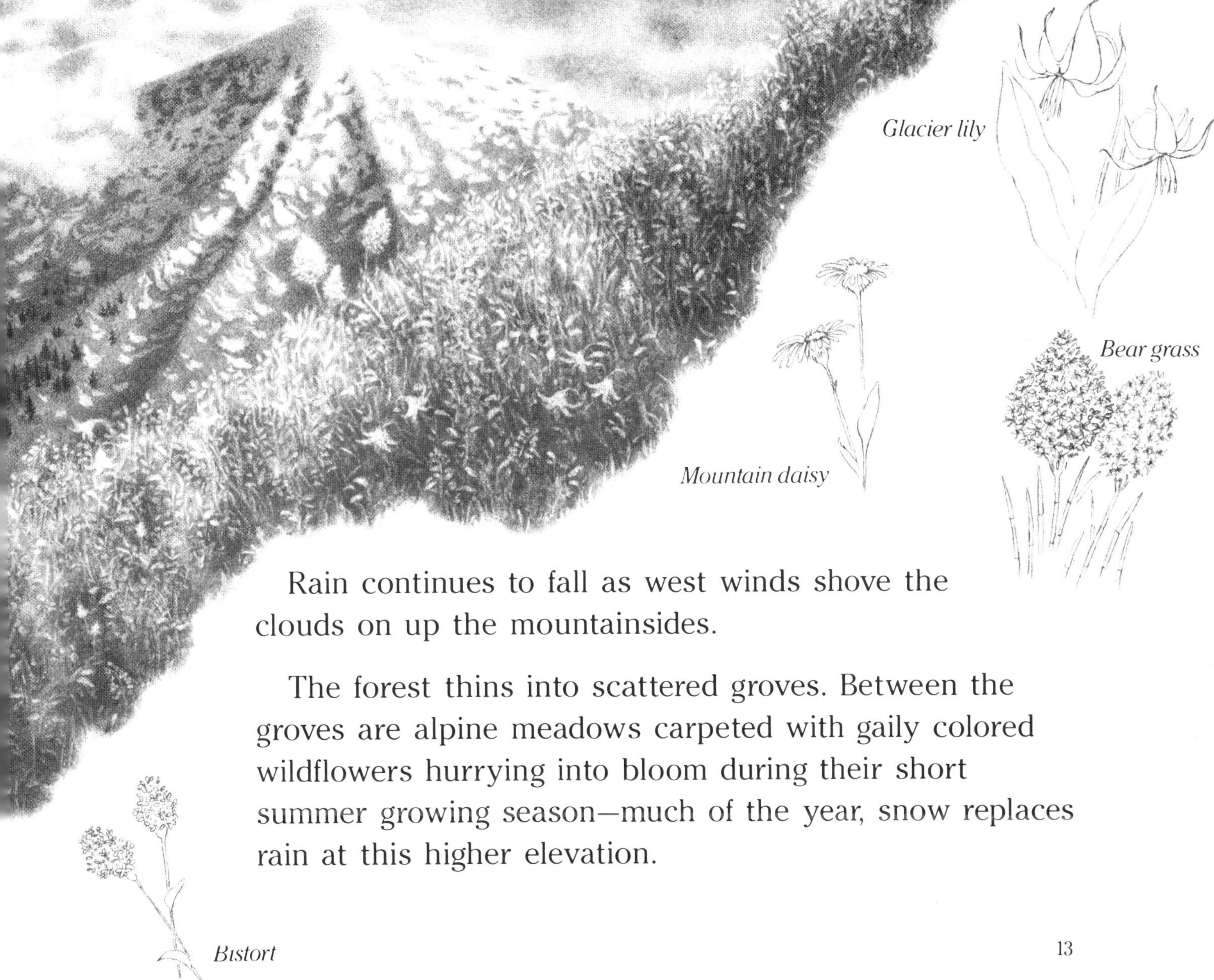

Rain continues to fall as west winds shove the clouds on up the mountainsides.

The forest thins into scattered groves. Between the groves are alpine meadows carpeted with gaily colored wildflowers hurrying into bloom during their short summer growing season—much of the year, snow replaces rain at this higher elevation.

Upslope from the alpine meadows lie fields of snow
and ice. Here, where the jagged mountain peaks wear
a blanket of white all year long, the clouds dump
nearly all the rest of their moisture.

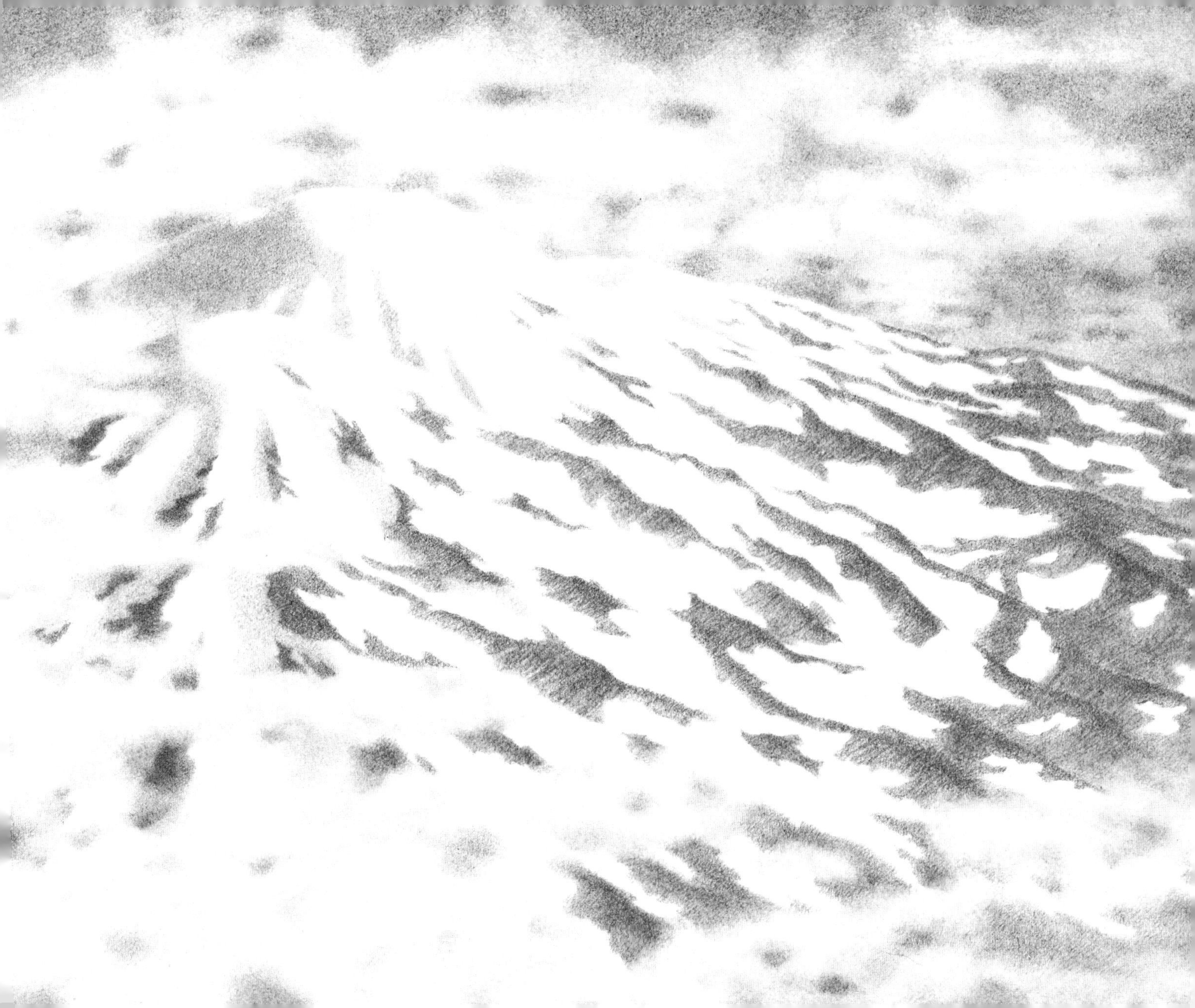

Meltwaters gushing from beneath the ice-and-snow
fields quickly come together to form rushing
streams. The frigid waters race downhill
through the alpine meadows, rain forests,
and sand dunes to join the ocean
from which they came.

Wrung dry by the cold air, the thin white clouds that are left leave the peaks behind. They glide above the more sparsely forested slopes on the eastern side of the mountains.

Then they slide down over the valleys. They will need to travel a great distance before warming enough again to grow and darken with moisture.

These valleys on the leeward side of the mountains
receive scant rainfall from the nearly moistureless
clouds passing overhead. While almost 200 inches of
rain and snow fall each year on the ocean side of the
mountain peaks, the land on the side away from the sea
gets less than 20 inches of rain yearly.

The valleys lie in what is called the "rain shadow"
of the mountains. Just as a tree casts a shadow that
keeps the sun from the ground, so the mountains spread
a shadow of dryness, keeping rain from the valleys.

How different everything looks in the rain shadow! The land is colored with grays, browns, and yellows, instead of shades of green. Gone are the dense forests found on the ocean side of the mountains. In their place are rolling hills and flatlands speckled with shrublike sagebrush.

Scattered between the bushes of sagebrush are prickly pear cacti and patches of bunchgrass. These plants are well suited to this land of little rainfall. Each is adapted in special ways to living in the arid climate of the rain shadow.

During long dry spells the bunchgrass may die off except for its root system. Then, with the first rain, new blades of grass spring up from the roots.

The stems of the prickly pear cacti are covered with a waxy material. Slender spines take the place of leaves. Both of these features help protect the plants from loss of water by evaporation.

The dusty gray sagebrush is covered with little hairs that trap and hold moisture. To help conserve this precious water the plant may shed its small leaves during periods of extremely dry weather.

There is not enough moisture in the rain shadow to support great amounts of plant growth. So little rain falls that farmers must dig irrigation canals to get enough water to grow crops. With these canals they capture some of the water from the rivers that flow into the valleys from the nearby mountains.

Rain shadows are found in many other places around the world. One of the wettest spots on earth is on the windy side of Mount Waialeale on the Hawaiian island of Kauai. Nearly 500 inches of rain falls there each year, and yet just a few miles away in the rain shadow of that mountain there is less than 20 inches of rain yearly. Only the mountain separates these two areas, and yet they are so different.

Joshua trees in the Great American Desert

Some of the driest places, including the Patagonian Desert in South America and the Great American Desert of North America, lie in rain shadows, cut off from rain-carrying winds by lofty mountains.

Mountains, wind, water, sun—
all are needed to produce a rain shadow.
Sun heating the air. Water evaporating,
rising, cooling, condensing into clouds.
Winds moving and forcing the clouds inland.
Huge mountains, tall enough to grip the
clouds, holding them, wringing them nearly
dry. Then the valleys that lie beyond the
mountains will be the arid lands we call
rain shadows.